WELLS
A Pictorial History

Aerial view of Wells.

WELLS
A Pictorial History

Tony Scrase

Phillimore

1992

Published by
PHILLIMORE & CO LTD.
Shopwyke Hall, Chichester, Sussex

ISBN 0 85033 814 X

Printed and bound in Great Britain by
BIDDLES LTD.,
Guildford, Surrey

To my wife

List of Illustrations

Frontispiece: Aerial view of Wells

Acknowledgements

Many persons and bodies have helped me to make this book possible. The following have made vital contributions, without which there would have been no book: Lesley-Ann Kerr, Curator Wells Museum, who has been unfailingly helpful to all my requests and has devoted considerable time to my visits; Colin Peacock of Wells, to whom I am triply indebted for all his splendid prints from the Phillips negatives and his putting at my disposal his knowledge of both Phillips collection and of the Phillips firm and the other photographers in Wells; Bob Steadman, technician, Bristol Polytechnic, for modern acceptable copies of a variety of old materials; and Margaret Thompson and Barbara Fortune of Bristol Polytechnic for word processing.

Pictures are reproduced by permission of the following: R. K. Blencowe, 125, 126 and 142; The Warden and Fellows, New College, Oxford, 1; Madeline Paul, 24, 95, 118, 124, 128, 133, 139, 151-4, 165, 166 and 168-70. Eric Purchase, photographer, 9 High Street, Wells, 171 and 172; Warwick Rodwell, 12; Somerset Archaeological and Natural History Society, 10, 16, 36, 84 and 109; Somerset Health Authority, 49, the Master and Fellows, Trinity College, Cambridge, 20; David Tudway Quilter, 61, 62, 74-7, 79, 97, 98 and 160; the Dean and Chapter of Wells, 29-35 and 81; Wells Museum and the Trustees of the Phillips Collection, 13, 15, 17-19, 21, 27, 37, 45-8, 52-4, 58, 59, 64, 65, 69-71, 73, 85, 87-8, 90, 91, 92, 93, 96, 99, 100, 101, 103-5, 112, 113, 116, 122, 129-32, 134, 135, 137-8, 140, 141, 143, 144, 146-8, 154-9, 161-3, 164 and 167; Wells Museum (for material from other collections), 3, 22, 44, 51, 55, 60, 66, 78, 83, 110, 114, 120, 136, 173 and 174; West Air Photography, frontispiece.

The modern maps, numbers 111 and 127, were prepared by Paul Dyke, technician, Bristol Polytechnic.

The following have all provided help and advice whenever requested: David Bromwich, Hon. Librarian, Somerset Archaeological and Natural History Society; Jean Imray, former City Archivist, Wells and organiser of the Wells local history study group; Frances Neale, Hon. Archivist, Wells Cathedral; and William Smith, City Archivist, Wells.

Introduction

Wells stands on a narrow bench separating the two major physical features of the locality, the Mendips and the Somerset 'moors' or levels. Visually the high steep-sided plateau of the Mendips is dominant. It consists mainly of Carboniferous Limestone with a fairly uniform surface at around 800 ft. above sea level. The whole system has been subject to faulting and thrusting, and Wells is at a point of transition. Westward the hills have a simple and impressive single face, but to the east the geological movements have produced a series of outlying ridges at Worminster Sleight, Dulcote and Lyatt Hill.

This contrast is important for Wells. It means that it is located at a point where valleys offer a relatively easy ascent from the bench into the eastern Mendips. But more importantly the faults, in effect, trap a large volume of ground water and divert it westwards, thus contributing to the vigour of the springs of Wells. The insertion of dyes into water entering swallet holes on the limestone revealed a catchment forming a quadrant, extending from Upper Milton on the north, by way of Haydon to Windsor Hill behind Shepton Mallet. (See W. I. Staunton, 'The Ancient Springs, Streams and Watercourses of the City of Wells', *Wells Natural History and Archaeological Society Report*, 1988.) The bedrock of the bench is of late Triassic and Liassic materials which once covered the flanks of Mendip. It is now overlain with erosion-transported materials of various ages, the most recent being from the last Ice Age. The resultant mix gives fertile soils. These, with abundant springs and a sheltered southern aspect make the bench especially favoured for agriculture. Today it is noted for strawberries, and it carried vineyards in the Middle Ages.

To the south and west lie the levels which do not exceed 20 ft. above sea level and whose surface is broken only by a few chains of low hills or 'island' sites like Glastonbury or Wedmore. The geology is recent, comprising peat with bands of estuarine clay representing periodic incursions by the sea. The whole was subject to periodic flooding until the drainage works of modern times.

Wells is excellently sited to exploit the contrasting resources of these zones. This economic potential is increased by the mineral wealth of the Mendips. The silver, lead and zinc ores are best known, but there is also iron, fullers earth, lime and a variety of building stones. In addition the levels contribute peat as a fuel or gardening aid. It seems to have been the springs, however, which provided the first focus of human activity. Dr. Warwick Rodwell's excavations, from 1978-80, to their west in the Camery revealed a long sequence before the first recorded event, around A.D.700. As might be expected these particularly large and copious springs have attracted attention for a very long period. His earliest finds were arrowheads and flints demonstrating the presence of prehistoric people. Above these came Roman remains – pottery and building materials. The latter were so abundant as to indicate a building nearby. Possibly a villa is inaccessible under the east end of the cathedral.

By the late Roman times or immediately afterwards the springs were attracting religious veneration, so a mausoleum was built to the west of the spring subsequently dedicated to St Andrew. By the eighth century, and possibly before, burials were being made around the mausoleum. It is clear, therefore, that when King Ine of Wessex established a minster church at Wells in *c.*700 it was not set out on a virgin site. A minster would have been a missionary centre providing priests to preach in the surrounding area. The substantial outparish of St Cuthbert (the largest in Somerset) is a relic of its extensive sphere of influence. The minster presumably lay to the west of the mausoleum and under the modern cloisters, where the Anglo-Saxon cathedral was situated. It was in 909 that King Edward the Elder reorganised the over-large Wessex bishopric into county-based dioceses. Wells was selected as the seat of the new bishop of Somerset. The mausoleum had been replaced by a mortuary chapel, and in the 10th century it, in turn, gave place to a two-cell building dedicated to St Mary. This was subsequently linked to the apse of the cathedral. There has thus developed a linear pattern comprising, from east to west, St Andrew's spring, the mortuary chapel or later St Mary's, and the cathedral. As Rodwell pointed out, this alignment is continued by Market Place, High Street and St Cuthbert Street. Furthermore, these only form the southern side of a regular and approximately rectangular layout. Chamberlain Street forms the northern parallel while Portway, Priest Row, Union Street and Sadler Street provide the cross-links.

This pattern is anchored on the first cathedral and resembles a number of Anglo-Saxon planned towns, but the need for such an ambitious scheme is a puzzle. This is because we have no written evidence of urban functions at Wells before *c.*1160. There are other clues to the size of pre-conquest Wells. The dedications of both the parish church and the former free chapel in Southover are Anglo-Saxon, being respectively to St Cuthbert and St Etheldreda. A Norman bishop would have regarded such names as obscure and uncouth. They must date from before 1066 and the need for cathedral, parish church and chapel clearly reflects a settlement of some size.

By the time of Domesday Book the bishop held extensive estates throughout Somerset. Of these the manor of Wells was the richest with, for example, nine mills. It formed a great estate stretching from the heights of the Mendips southwards to the levels. Unfortunately the Domesday entry is for the entire manor so we have no separate picture of the 11th-century settlement.

The first Norman appointed bishop, John de Villula, held the see from 1088 to 1122 and moved his seat to Bath. This was in nominal accordance with the post-conquest decree requiring bishoprics to move from villages to towns, but the real attraction was that he could augment his titles and income by also holding the office of Abbot of Bath. Twenty-five years of neglect followed but his second successor, Robert of Lewes, took more interest in Wells. He recovered lands still held by Bishop John's kinsman, reorganised the canons and initiated some repair or rebuilding of the cathedral. About 1160 he also granted the town its first charter. The next bishop, Reginald, granted no less than three charters to the town and commenced the reconstruction of the cathedral. Robert had allowed the town the right to hold weekly markets and three fairs per year. Reginald added a fourth fair. His successor, Savaric, obtained the first royal charter from King John, which granted the status of a free borough and a fifth, and final, fair.

In 1206 Jocelyn Trotman was elected Bishop of Bath: the monks of Bath were probably remiss in agreeing to his selection. He was born in Launcherley some two miles south of Wells, in the outparish, and he quickly returned the diocesan administration to his home town. There were practical reasons for the move too, as Bath was an awkwardly peripheral site for the administration of both the see and the bishop's estates. It was as a consequence of the move that Jocelyn built the first stage of the palace and created the park. To make the park, a minor road from Southover to Wellesley was closed and the major roads towards Glastonbury and Shepton Mallet shifted outwards. The former was moved to the west and the latter to the east, where Tor Street was created as part of the realignment. This seems to have been the last major adjustment to the town's road pattern for 600 years. Certainly all the roads shown on Simes' bird's-eye plan of 1735 were in existence by the second half of the 13th century. The park's creation has had a continuing impact on the town's form. Northward growth was hindered by the slopes of Mendip, and Jocelyn had added a barrier on the south. As a result, the medieval town already had a relatively shallow (north-south) breadth compared with its length from east to west. Modern development has tended to increase this characteristic.

Jocelyn was unable, however, to enjoy his creations in tranquillity. He was amongst the bishops who pronounced the papal bull excommunicating King John, and had to flee the country. During his exile, work on the cathedral halted, but Jocelyn returned after John's submission and survived to see the new cathedral consecrated. Once the new building was operating, the Anglo-Saxon cathedral was demolished and the cloisters were built across the site. Only St Mary's chapel survived, linked to the east side of the cloisters. It was probably preserved because of some tradition concerning the venerability of its site, as it must have sat rather incongruously beside the new buildings. The new cathedral was realigned by 12 degrees, so the chapel was noticeably oblique to the adjacent cloister and cathedral walls.

Wells was to remain the diocesan centre from Jocelyn's time. Bath had to be content with primacy in the bishop's title. The town then entered its greatest period of prosperity, being in the later Middle Ages the largest town in Somerset and making a brief appearance in the national list of the top 40 towns. This well-being partly reflects the people drawn by the combination of cathedral and bishop's seat, on diocesan business, pilgrimage, business generated by the bishop's vast estates or major role in local administration and justice, or as a consequence of successive bishops holding great offices of state.

In addition the town developed its own functions. As we have seen, it was a natural centre for the exchange of the produce of three contrasting zones. It also developed a substantial textile industry based on Mendip sheep, abundant water and nearby fuller's earth deposits. The records reveal the early appearance and substantial number of fulling mills. The name Tucker Street is also a reminder of this influence.

Prosperity, however, did not equate with harmony. There was endemic conflict between the bishops and a citizen body eager for greater self-government: the most acute crisis occurred in the period 1340-3. In 1341 the burgesses obtained a charter, for £40, from the king, granting them rights of justice and self-government. They were also allowed to levy a rate to build a town wall. In January the following year, the grant was quashed by the Court of Chancery as it had ignored the bishop's rights. Demonstrations and boycotts followed. Bishop Ralph of Shrewsbury returned to the Courts and the principal dissidents amongst the citizens were fined £3,000. The most tangible results of this crisis were royal grants authorising walls to protect first the bishop's palace and then the cathedral precinct. Subsequently, in 1400 a later generation of burgesses obtained a royal charter which recognised them as a corporate body.

These rights of the citizenry were restricted to an area to the west of the cathedral. It and its surroundings formed a separate jurisdiction – the Liberty of St Andrew. To the east of the cathedral was a suburb known in the medieval period as 'Byestewalles' and subsequently as East Wells. Administratively this formed part of the bishop's Manor of Wells and the out-parish of St Cuthbert. It was only incorporated into the city following the 1835 Municipal Reform Act. Progressively, the pattern of development diverged and the Liberty of St Andrew took on a different appearance to both the city and suburb. In these last two, processes were at work which tended to split house plots into smaller units and to make boundaries more complex. The pressures included the demand for premises on commercially desirable roads, the need to accommodate an increasing population, the demand for smaller shop and cottage units and the tradition by which one third of a property was allocated to a widow as her dower. In the Liberty, property passed into the hands of the Church and was assigned to the dean, cathedral officers and canons for their residences. They were not subject to the same economic and family pressures. Plots remained large and buildings more spacious. If there was change it was more likely to be the amalgamation of plots. The sole exception was the Vicars' Close, laid out *c*.1345 to accommodate the vicars choral, and occupying the site of a single canonical house.

By the end of the Middle Ages, Wells had three other religious foundations. The earliest was the Hospital of St John the Baptist in Southover, first endowed *c*.1220 by Bishop Jocelyn and Hugh, his brother, who was successively Archdeacon of Wells and Bishop of Lincoln. By 1430 a house for chantry priests, the College of Montroy, was provided at the corner of The Liberty and College Road. Shortly after, in 1436, Bubwith's Almshouse was built.

One general trend was apparent in the medieval property market – the tendency for property to move into institutional hands. The reason for this was piety: property was bequeathed to secure prayers for the souls of the donors and their kin. The dean and chapter, hospital and vicars choral all benefited greatly, and the town corporation as trustee of the parish church also did well. The College and Almshouses as latecomers had less time to develop a substantial income from rents. By the eve of the Reformation, though, all of the Liberty of St Andrew, nearly 85 per cent of the City properties and some 50 per cent of the suburb, were in institutional hands.

Wells did not suffer greatly in the long depression that followed the Black Death, but the national loss of population was indicated by some recession in the built-up areas. This was most apparent on College Road and New Street where houses had once extended north to the area of the modern Bristol Hill, Old Bristol Road, Ash Lane and College Road intersections. Other streets had long-lasting gaps, for example Moniers Lane, a development of *c*.1343 which lay to the east of Union Street, and dwindled to a few cottages. But well-placed sites could still be developed. In 1451 Bishop Bekynton launched the largest secular development of the Middle Ages in Wells. This was the New Works, where the southern fringe of St Andrew's churchyard abutted what is now Market Place. As part of the same process three houses were built south of Brown's Gate on Sadler Street. These straddled the precinct wall and incorporated a further strip of the churchyard.

The 16th century was to be a low point in the town's fortunes. It began with two absentee bishops, first the Italian Hadrian de Castello (1504-18) and then the great Wolsey (1518-23), who removed both expenditure and activity from Wells. Then in the 1520s the textile trade experienced a general slump and on top of this came the Reformation. The hospital, College of Montroy and chapel were dissolved, and manors and estates belonging to the bishop were lost: manors held by the bishop of Bath and Wells fell from 26 to eight. Visitors and the bishop's expenditure fell in proportion, and the results were apparent throughout the town fabric. By mid-century Moniers Lane was a vacant plot. In 1550-1 the Corporation, faced by vacant sites and dilapidated properties, had to reassess its rents, which resulted in a 13 per cent fall in income. Other corporate landlords had similar problems.

After 1550 the situation began to improve. Diocesan business stabilised at a new level. The Mendip lead mines became increasingly important from the late 16th century, and new textile industries also appeared. Linen was important by the early 17th century and when Defoe visited the town *c.*1720 it was chiefly noted for the manufacture of stockings. Again the market maintained its viability.

Once the crisis had passed the town council began to regain its confidence. The town had held on to its properties and no longer had to support the chantry and obit priests at St Cuthbert's. Furthermore, rents soon improved and by the 1580s yielded more than before the 1550-1 crisis. By the 1570s the council was confident enough to skirmish with Bishop Berkeley, and in 1571 meat and fish shambles were built in the middle of High Street, ignoring the Bishop's rights. Next year they built a new town hall over part of the shambles. In 1589 the impoverished Bishop Godwin agreed (for suitable payment) a new charter giving most of the long-sought rights of self-government. The new powers to hold courts led to the building of a city gaol in 1606, which was located at what is now the *City Arms*. There were already prisons maintained by both the bishop and the chapter.

During this period, from *c.*1550, the nature of trade began to change. Traders covered a wider area, and networks became more informal, fewer deals being struck in the open market. It is hardly surprising in these circumstances that inns began to flourish: 'The Elizabethan and Stuart inn has no exact counterpart in the modern world. It was the hotel, the bank, the warehouse, the exchange, the scrivener's office and the market-place of many a private trader'. (Alan Everitt, 'The Marketing of Agricultural Produce', *Agrarian History of England and Wales*, Vol. 4, 1967). Wells is well provided with licensed premises today but they are only a remnant of those which flourished from *c.*1550-1750, especially around the High Street/Sadler Street/Market Place intersection, and the boundaries of the Liberty. Just before 1700 Sadler Street contained the *Swan, Flower de Luce, Hart's Head, Mitre* and *White Horse*; Market Place, the *Crown*, the south side of High Street, west to Guard House Lane, the *Red Lion, White Hart, George, Katherine Wheel, Bell, Hare and Hounds* and *Christopher*, while the north side, west to Union Street, added the *Company of Taylors, Hole in the Wall, Star, Queen's Arms, Ship* and *King's Head*. After 1750 the number of inns declined gradually although there was a brief explosion in the number of beerhouses after the relaxation of licensing laws in 1830.

By the mid-17th century Wells was also becoming a resort for local gentry or those who aspired to genteel status. The journal of the physician Claver Morris depicts this new social order. Morris sat as a Commissioner, held meetings of his music society, read the news, saw plays, dealt in property, tried to influence elections or simply dined and drank in the *Mitre, George* or *Crown*. It was during this period that the easternmost house in Cathedral Green was converted into an assembly room, while a small theatre was built in Priest Row.

As Wells was no longer important enough to support wealthy merchants, and the bishop had withdrawn from municipal affairs, resident gentry began to fill the political void during the late 17th and early 18th centuries. In the years on either side of 1700 the Coward family and their son-in-law, the Hon. George Hamilton, exerted a major influence from their mansion on the south of Chamberlain Street. They were challenged and ousted, however, by the Tudway family, whose wealth came from their plantations in Antigua, and whose status was to find physical expression. In 1755 Charles Tudway bought the old College of Montroy premises and replaced its buildings in 1758 with the substantial Georgian house subsequently known as The Cedars. In addition many of the grander houses in Chamberlain Street and New Street were rebuilt for the family's dowagers and younger sons. Milton Lodge and Stoberry House were also acquired from other local gentry.

In the 1760s the Tudways quarrelled with the Recorder over the conduct of an election, and provoked a bout of litigation. Clement Tudway then took steps to consolidate his family influence: Wells was to be the Tudway's pocket borough until 1828. The 1794 Directory epitomises it: 'The influence prevailing in this city is that of Clement Tudway, Esq., one of its present representatives. This gentleman has a sufficient interest to procure a return for himself without expense and the Corporation, etc. compliment some particular friend or neighbour with the other seat'. It would be easy to project this picture onto municipal affairs and assume a period of inaction, but in fact the Corporation became increasingly involved in urban improvement. In 1754 the stalls which had cluttered High Street were relocated in a yard behind the rebuilt *Queen's Arms*. Part of the Middle Row was also removed, and in 1768 the remainder of Middle Row was demolished to clear High Street.

In 1779 the canonical house on the south of Market Place was acquired from the bishop and its occupier, the archdeacon of Wells. Its front garden was thrown into Market Place and the house was replaced by a new town hall. Town administration had finally completed a slow migration from locations in and around St Cuthbert's to a site by the cathedral. As part of the same transaction the Corporation acquired the bishop's prerogatives in the town market. This resolved the last cause of historic conflict.

In 1821-2 the corner between High Street and Sadler Street was improved. The last act of the unreformed council, in 1835, was to acquire Palace Mill and adjacent houses from the bishop. Most of the site was then used to build a new market hall (now the post office). To finance this over a third of the council estate was sold. This and the associated sales by the bishop signalled the end of the traditional property market dominated by institutional estates.

In 1839 the reformed council further enlarged the Market Place by acquiring and demolishing a house to the east of modern no. 10. But the chief vehicle of change was now the Wells Turnpike Trustees. In the 1830s they improved the main approaches to the town. On the south, Wet Lane, which was 12 ft. wide at its narrowest point, was widened to create Broad Street. Its alignment was continued across the former Hospital grounds, making Priory Road into the new approach from Glastonbury. In the north, the complex set of junctions at the head of New Street was rationalised and Bristol traffic was directed to the modern main road and away from the steep and tortuous Old Bristol Road.

Much of this activity was necessary to modernise Wells for the age of the stage coach, but it also seems to reflect an anxiety that Wells was declining, if only in relative terms. Although other towns were experiencing rapid growth in both population and economy, in Wells, like most of western England, the textile trade was nearly dead. The early 19th century saw a brief attempt to specialise in silk but this failed. The economic base was dwindling. Population growth echoed this, only increasing in line with national trends, and the town only began to expand significantly in the last quarter of the century. Until this time housing demand was satisfied by the use of the backland of the long narrow plots which had been in existence since the Middle Ages. The results were courts approached by an alley or arch and with a row of cottages with windows on one side only. Such windows frequently faced the blank wall of the next court. The majority of these dwellings have been cleared, designated slums, since World War Two.

The Victorian age saw further dramatic changes in patterns of marketing and shopping, largely resulting from the new mobility granted by the railways. The most important towns had good main line connections. The railway arrived rather late in Wells and in the unsatisfactory form of three branch lines. The first company to show an interest was the Somerset Central Railway, soon to become part of the Somerset & Dorset Joint, but it hesitated while considering routes eastwards. As a result the East Somerset Railway, which was building a line from what was then the G.W.R.'s Weymouth Branch at Witham to Shepton Mallet, was approached. In 1856 an extension to Wells was agreed, and this provoked the Somerset Central to push on, with their branch from Glastonbury arriving in 1859. The East Somerset followed in 1862 and the rival stations faced each other across Priory Road. Finally the Bristol and Exeter Railway built a branch from Yatton via Cheddar, terminating at Tucker Street, which was reached in 1870. Despite early nominal independence the East Somerset and Bristol and Exeter both belonged to the G.W.R. system. Rivalry with the S.& D.J.R. precluded co-operation at Wells, and for a time the separate termini had their own engine sheds and turntables. In 1878 a level-crossing was built at Priory Road and a spur from the S.& D.J.R. station to Tucker Street was completed. This allowed the G.W.R. to close the East Somerset station and to work trains from Yatton to Witham. But they did not stop at their rival's Priory Road until 1934, by which time it was too late to exploit any potential as a minor junction. The town now had only the twin roles of cathedral town and local market centre, together with a handful of manufacturing enterprises, notably the making of uniforms and brushes.

From our point of view this was fortunate, as it allowed the preservation of much of the fabric and pattern of late medieval and early modern Wells. There were, of course, changes. The town received the usual technological and public health improvements – gas-works, street-lighting, a sewerage system and piped water supplies. There were also significant changes to buildings. The medieval Hospital of St John was demolished in 1858 to make way for the Central School (now itself replaced). The 17th-century Llewellyn Almshouses were rebuilt in the 1880s on an enlarged site incorporating several neighbouring houses. Bubwith's Almshouses were also substantially modernised. The character of the town was changing, as the wealth of the resident gentry diminished and new political ideas began to broaden the franchise. The sale of the institutional estates saw the rise of small landlords and owner-occupiers. Buildings expressed this wider spread of wealth.

Religion also experienced a revival at this time. The first dissenting chapel had been built in Southover in 1738, and the number of chapels increased in the new century. By 1845 the theatre had been converted. Then in 1861, a new Anglican church of St Thomas was provided for East Wells. Finally in 1874 the former mansion of the Cowards and George Hamilton was acquired for a Catholic convent. A church was built to its west, and a school was sited where its stables had fronted Union Street. The church is built on top of any remains of medieval Moniers Lane. This religious revival also produced a strong temperance movement whose members bought several inns and closed them: the *Mitre* vanished in this way and the *Red Lion* was converted to a temperance hotel for two decades. Other popular drinking houses were challenged by adjacent coffee rooms.

Compared with the explosion of urban growth elsewhere Wells grew relatively slowly in the late 18th and 19th centuries. In 1640 the borough had had a population of just under 2,000, while the Liberty of St Andrew had about 180. By the time of the first census, in 1801 the figures stood at 2,229 and 268 respectively. By 1901 these had increased to 3,702 and 361. In 1971 an enlarged town area and the Liberty had a population of 8,855.

Early 20th-century Wells was in many ways conditioned by long traditions. The horror of World War One took its toll on Wells, as on the rest of the country: there was the usual loss of the male population to the services, and subsequent heavy casualties. In addition The Cedars was converted to a military hospital, so that the sight of sick and wounded became a familiar one; and there were occasional military funerals.

The inter-war years witnessed more changes. Motor vehicles became increasingly familiar. There were more tourists and some new housing, including the first council houses. The pressure to build was not great enough, however, to create problems of uncoordinated, badly placed or ribbon development.

World War Two had less direct impact than its predecessor. A contemporary slogan was 'Britain can take it'. Those left at home had to cope with strict rations, blackout, and heavy taxation. There were also frequent campaigns to raise even more money to support the forces, or to collect useful materials (see illustrations 151-4). The only direct impact the war made in the Wells area was in the period after Dunkirk when the Somerset levels were considered as a suitable landing place for gliders and paratroops. As a result a defence line was constructed from Coxley, across the Park and on to the ridge at Lyatt. The defence consisted of anti-tank trenches and other obstacles popularly called dragons' teeth, which were supplemented by strong points known as pill-boxes. Examples of these survive in various rural settings while the trenches revealed neolithic and Roman remains.

The post-war years saw a determined effort to improve housing. Most of the courts were closed during the 1950s and '60s and subsequently demolished, new council estates providing better housing. Other planning proposals were rather more controversial: in 1949 quarrying at Dulcote Hill became an issue. In 1952 the City Council proposed to demolish nos. 8 and 10 Market Place (Phillips' premises) to open up views to the restored *Crown*. This controversy brought the local Preservation Society to the fore, a pivotal argument being whether William Penn, the Quaker, had preached from the upper window of no. 8 or from a window of the *Crown*. The Corporation failed.

More generally the years since 1950 have seen a burgeoning tourist trade and unparalleled physical growth. New housing estates are associated with the growth of commuting, and the demand for retirement homes in pleasant locations. More recently this good environment has created fresh pressures. In the absence of some compelling link such as a motorway, car-borne shoppers seem to prefer an attractive town and therefore Wells is drawing the interest of retailing chains. Similarly businesses are searching out surroundings where their executives will be content, and where they can attract and hold key workers. All of the above may be seen as arguably beneficial effects of the internal combustion engine, but Wells faces the unresolved problem of sheer weight of traffic. Cars and lorries, the latter including many from the quarries of the Mendips, pour through the town's historic core, making a series of one-way streets necessary. All this conflicts with both agreeable shopping and appreciation of the historic legacy. One attempt to provide relief roads foundered in intense controversy, and at the time of writing this problem has still to be resolved.

1. The earliest view: the cathedral, palace and adjacent areas, *c.*1463. Thomas Chaundler, an author and native of Wells, presents one of his books to his patron, Bishop Bekynton. The palace moat, walls and drawbridge are the most recognisable features. Note the profusion of watercourses and bridges in the street. Presumably this area is now occupied by the Market Place.

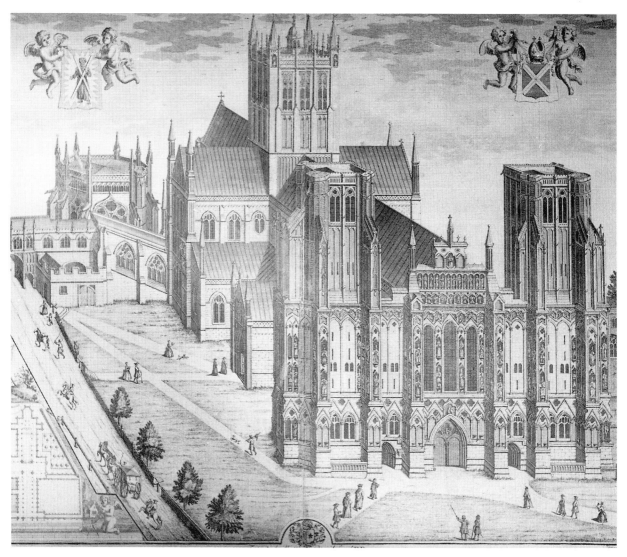

2. The cathedral from the west, *c.*1730, showing the west front and the chapter house complex. The cathedral was dedicated in 1239 and the chapter house started soon after, but financial difficulties delayed completion until 1309. This view shows considerable activity. Note the turnstile-like gates. These were first documented in 1502 and were known as whirligogs.

3. The great spring or well which gave the town its name and was the focus of early activity. Beyond are the lady chapel and east end of the cathedral, which are here duplicated by reflections in Phillips' study. The Anglo-Saxon and Norman cathedral lay to the south (left) of its successor, being aligned with the spring (see pictures 11 and 12).

4. Some of nearly 300 statues on the west front. Thomas Phillips first photographed them during the 1871 restoration. This was a major feat and he long displayed appreciative letters from Ruskin and others in his shop window. Restoration in the 1980s revealed paint specks on the figures, so they were originally coloured.

5. The nave, looking towards the massive scissors-arches built 1338-48. The tower was raised to about double its original height in 1313, and as a result the two western tower-piers began to sink into the soft ground. Master mason William Joy redistributed the load by incorporating these arches and flying buttresses into the fabric, and thus prevented the tower's collapse.

6. Inside the cathedral the nave capitals are a treasure house of medieval carving. This photograph by Phillips shows a fox making off with a goose. A peasant looks on in dismay, his cudgel and stone useless. They are on the seventh pillar, north side. Elsewhere there are 11 studies on the theme of toothache!

7. Further Phillips details. Here the carving is in wood on the misericords (folding seats in the chancel). There were originally 65 of these carvings and they only became well known after Phillips photographed them. The two illustrated show a bat and a man waking and stretching.

8. The interior face of the 14th-century clock. The outer dial has 24 hours marked, with a sun indicating the hour. On the second a star shows the minute. The third gives the date in the lunar month, while the small circle shows the phase of the moon. The knights rotate (and tilt) at the quarters.

9. The cloisters looking east. These were built over the site of the earlier cathedral. Little remains of Jocelyn's work as they were rebuilt in the 15th century when upper floors were added to the eastern and western walks. The former (seen here) was to house the library and the latter the grammar and choristers' schools (subsequently combined in Wells Cathedral School).

10. The chapter house steps have been the subject of innumerable picture postcards and photographs. This engraving of *c.*1830 is their predecessor. If it is accurate most of the wear to the steps has occurred in the last 150 years, but this is doubtful. The architectural detail seems correct, but either the height is exaggerated or the figures are about three feet tall!

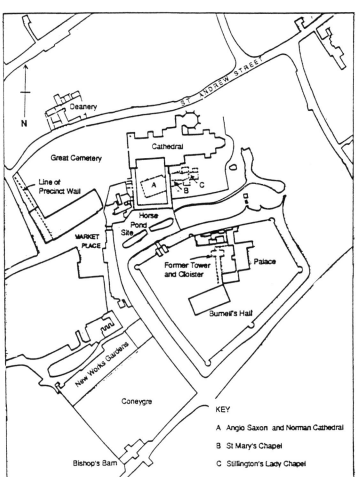

11. Plan of the cathedral and its surrounding area, illustrating the relationship of the present cathedral with its predecessor and other lost features. These comprise the lady chapel off the cloister, the palace cloister and tower, the horsepool and the precinct wall. See also pictures 12, 14, 16, 23 and 107.

KEY

A Anglo Saxon and Norman Cathedral

B St Mary's Chapel

C Stillington's Lady Chapel

12. Dr. Warwick Rodwell's excavations of 1978-80 in the Camery, showing the foundations of successive chapels off the cloisters. Stillington's 15th-century chapel (see picture 14) is represented by the outer walls. The lower wall at an angle to these reveals the Anglo-Saxon alignment. Burials can be dated by which alignment they follow.

13.   The cathedral library, *c.*1900. This was
a bequest of Bishop Bubwith. It was built in
two stages, from 1425-33. With a length of
over 160 ft. it is the largest medieval library
in England. The modern books and shelving
have now been removed and the ante-room
houses exhibitions. The benches and
shelving visible beyond date from 1686.

14.   The last medieval addition is lost. This
was Bishop Stillington's lady chapel, which
had replaced an earlier chapel, the last relic
of the first cathedral and its alignment. In
1552 this replacement was demolished by Sir
John Gates (Edward VI's collector of lead),
who plundered its roof. Its interior can be
judged by its rear wall which is preserved on
the cloisters.

15. The conduit house and th cathedral from the south-east The former was part of the works connected with Bishop Bekyngton's grant of a water supply to the citizens. See als picture 84 for the outlet in Market Place.

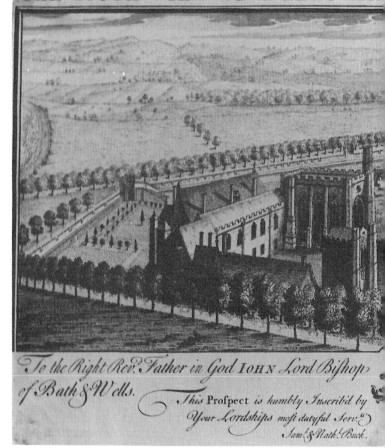

THE SOUTH VIEW OF WELLS PA

To the Right Rev.* Father in God IOHN Lord Bishop of Bath & Wells. This Prospect is humbly Inscrib'd by Your Lordships most dutyful Serv.* Sam.* & Nath.* Buck.

16. The bishop's palace, in 1773. The main contrasts with the more recent pictures are the subsequent disappearance of the tower at the end of the north range and the more complete state of the great hall, built in the late 13th century by Bishop Burnell (Edward I's chancellor). It was then a roofless shell but otherwise intact. The building across the moat was Palace Mill, demolished in 1835.

17. The palace, *c.*1890. The central range comprises Bishop Jocelyn's original house, with alterations by Ferrey, *c.*1850. It was built as an undercroft with hall above. To its right are the chapel and the ruins of Bishop Burnell's hall. The range to the left was mainly by Bekynton.

IN THE COUNTY OF SOMERSET.

This Palace has been y.ᵉ principal Place of Residence of y. Bᵖˢ. of Bath & Wells from y. 1ˢᵗ Erection of that See. Ralph de Salopia in y. Reign of H. Ed. 1. made y. Wall & Mote that surrounds it. Afterwards it was greatly improv'd by Bᵖ Beckinton, Bᵖ Burnell & other Succeeding Bᵖˢ. The great Hall built by Bᵖ Burnell was uncover'd in y. Reign of H. Ed. 6.ᵗʰ all y. rest of y. Buildings are yet entire, & in y. same good Repair as they were before the Reformation.

S & N Buck delin: et sculp: 1733

18.   Bishop Burnell's hall, *c.*1905. Sir John Gates had removed the roof of this building as well, but its ruinous appearance was mainly the work of Bishop Law (1824-45) who removed the south wall and two-storey porch to make a romantic garden feature and picnic site. He and his Victorian colleagues atoned by improving the grounds by tree planting. Note the early lawnmower.

19.   The north wing from across the moat, *c.*1895. A man-servant closely watches Phillips' activities. The wing was built to house the kitchens but since the Reformation it has provided domestic accommodation for bishops and their families. It was probably two of this building's chimneys which fell in the Great Storm of 1703, killing Bishop Kidder and his wife in their bed.

20. The palace interior, *c.*1464. Thomas Chaundler is shown presenting another of his books to Bekynton. The third figure is the Bishop's chaplain. This drawing is rare, as it was apparently drawn from life and it depicts a contemporary room. The geometric tiles contrast strongly with the vivid patterning of the throne canopy and wall hangings.

21. A Victorian view of the medieval long gallery. Over two centuries of the bishop's predecessors look down on the domestic clutter. They include the unfortunate Kidder and his immediate predecessor, the saintly Ken. Ken was one of the seven bishops sent to the tower by James II.

22.   The Bishop's Eye Gate from the palace side, in 1839. This was one of the three gates in the precinct wall commissioned by Bekynton *c.*1450 at a cost of 200 marks (about £130). Before that date there were only low arches. The most obvious alteration to this view has been the loss of the iron railings on the right.

23.   The green between the Palace and Bishop's Eye on market day. Today the space is tranquil, but when it contained the Horsepool (a figure-of-eight pond), before 1800, bishops complained regularly about the disturbance as traders watered their horses. Rubbish was also dumped here, and there would have been the clatter of Palace Mill.

24. The 15th-century bishop's barn is a backdrop here for the 1954 bowls team. The recreation ground (foreground) was the Coneygre where rabbits were kept. Grain from the bishop's manors was stored here until it was ground at Palace Mill, while venison came from the park, situated beyond the barn.

25. East Wells from the 1839 tithe map. It shows another adjunct to the Palace – the fishponds numbered 807 and 810: by the 1880s only one survived, and it had vanished by 1906. The map also shows the suburb's semi-rural nature with substantial gardens, orchards or home paddocks behind many properties. Something of this can be seen in picture 113.

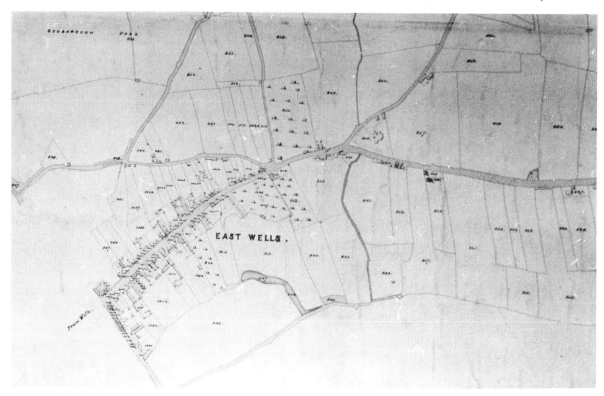

26.   Vicars' Close looking south, *c*.1900. The Close dates from 1348 and resulted from a grant by Bishop Ralph of Shrewsbury. This included provision of a hall for communal dining. The chimneys were heightened and embellished after 1465 following a bequest by **Bishop Bekynton**. On the right , no. 16 has been converted to what appears to be a Georgian house.

27.   The northern end of the Close showing the chapel, which was given by Bishop Bubwith. The chapel is a less simple structure than it appears. Because the Close employs false perspective, with the properties converging to the north while the road behind is at a slight angle, the pitch of the chapel's roof gradually changes to give the effect of being square on.

28. The Close has changed much through time, and even the gardens were not part of the original scheme. It was adapted further after the Reformation as vicars were permitted subsequently to marry. The doors and windows are mainly of 18th- or 19th-century date. The stonework, however, reveals earlier forms, for example, this doorway.

29. The Vicars' Hall. This is a wagon-roofed structure of 1348 with some additions, notably the oriel window on the left which was given by a vicar, Richard Pomeroy, c.1500. The fireplace and pulpit are commonly attributed to Hugh Sugar (d.1489) but the initials on it are actually KS. The Hall is remarkable for its furniture, especially the medieval benches and Restoration table.

30. A 15th-century breadbin in the Vicars' Hall. Presumably the day's bread ration for the 42 vicars was placed in here.

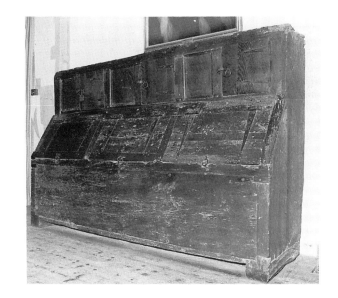

31. The kitchen's medieval drainage system. Washing-up water and other liquid waste was poured into this gully in the stone floor. It was then carried through the wall and emerged via a lead spout situated somewhat above head level! The system was used until recently. In modern times a look-out was stationed at the windows above the Chain Gate.

32. The kitchen adjoins the Vicars' Hall on the west. This view shows the fireplace and a stone sink now standing on the floor.

33. The tower carries the main stair from close to hall. The chequer and muniments room were on the top floor, while the treasury was tucked beneath the latter. Note the unglazed windows to the stairs and the narrow slits lighting the treasury. The chequer was glazed *c*.1912. Modern restoration has improved the road surface (contrast picture 26).

34. The chequer, where rents due to the vicars were paid, with the muniments room beyond. It is approached by a spiral stair from the hall. The treasury is below the muniments room, approached only by a hatch or a child-sized spiral stair. The chequer features original roof, shutters and fireplace.

35. The muniments room contains this remarkable survival – a 15th-century deed chest, which resembles a modern card index system. Each drawer would have contained rolls of parchment, and the ornamental nails would have held parchment labels identifying the property or estate. As it is handmade each drawer fits only its correct position.

36.   The Chain Gate in 1830. The physical fabric is virtually as shown below, but note the extra height of the wall around the cathedral and churchyard, together with the state of the road and the traffic. One wonders if the sheep were on their way from farm to farm, to market (see picture 84), or were going to crop the churchyard grass.

37.   The Chain Gate. This was the final part of Bekynton's benefaction to the Vicars Choral. It provided them with a covered way from their hall to the cathedral. The tracery and pinnacles of the bridge contrast with the plain front of the hall, apart from Pomeroy's oriel window. This is a study by Phillips of c.1890.

38. St Cuthbert's church, *c*.1874, photographed after the completion of various Victorian works. These included lowering the churchyard to reveal the building's line and to prevent damp in its interior. The stone pile outside shows the activity of the local roadman. Note how the pathway favours pedestrians at the road junction.

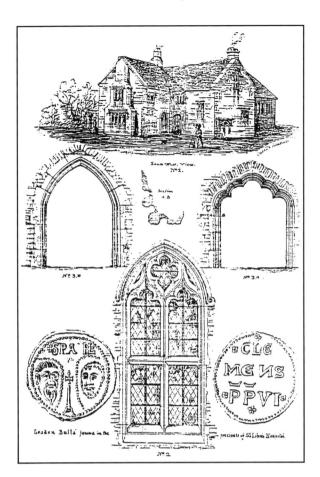

39. The Hospital of St John the Baptist was founded *c.*1220 by Bishop Jocelyn and his brother Hugh, Bishop of Lincoln. It was dissolved in 1539 but the main range survived until 1858. It was then cleared to form the site of the Central School. This general view and details were engraved by Serel in 1858.

40. The College of Montroy left even fewer records. Its general form can be appreciated in this extract from Simes' bird's-eye plan of 1735. It was completed by 1430, occupying what were the sites of the grammar school and another house. The college was dissolved in 1547, and was used as a private house until 1758, when it was demolished.

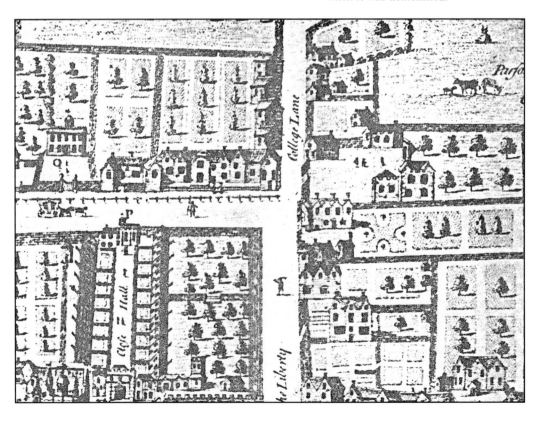

41. Bubwith's Almshouses from the east. This is a structure of 1436 with Victorian alterations, and was built to accommodate 24 persons. Entry was via the chapel at the east end from a porch which originally bridged the Ludbourne, a stream flowing along the south side of Chamberlain Street. The domestic accommodation is beyond the chapel.

42. Serious problems were created by the dissolution of the Hospital, and the abolition of commemorative services which often included distributions to the poor. After 1600 the need was tackled by private benefactions. First to act was Bishop Still, who provided accommodation for six behind Bubwith's range. Others followed his example. This view shows Victorian replacements to these additions.

43. A further four places were added in 1638 by Walter Bricke, a woollen draper. This is Bricke's Almshouse, which faces St Cuthbert's churchyard. A final four places were given in 1777 by Edward, son of Bishop Willes, who made the gift in his father's name. For convenience the whole complex was referred to as the Old Almshouse.

44. A resident outside Bricke's Almshouse, *c.*1900.

45. Llewellyn's Almshouses, Priest Row, *c.*1890. Alderman Llewellyn left £600 in his will dated 1604, and the bequest became operative in 1630. This is a Victorian replacement on an enlarged site which incorporates the last such bequest, Charles' Almshouse of 1828. The original double range of Llewellyn's Almshouses fitted between the front walls of the present buildings.

THE BLUE SCHOOLS, WELLS

PHILLIPS PHOTO

46. Charities also provided for education. Wells Charity School was founded in 1713, incorporating two earlier initiatives. In 1720 it commenced operations at St Andrew's Lodge (nos. 5 and 7 The Liberty). In 1820 it moved to the corner of Portway and Chamberlain Street. It acquired the name Blue School from its uniform. This is its third building, of 1895, sited further up Portway.

47. Priory Hospital, Glastonbury Road, *c.*1939. Provision for the poor in the 19th century was less compassionate. This was the Wells Union Workhouse from 1837 to 1930, and was subsequently converted to a hospital. Apart from the mills at Keward it was the first building to spread south-west of the medieval built-up area in Southover.

48. Mendip Hospital, *c.*1890. This was built as the Somerset County Lunatic Asylum in 1847. It occupied 36 acres and many patients were employed in farming and gardening for a mixture of therapeutic and economic reasons. The switch to 'care in the community' has recently made it redundant.

49. 'The Lunatics' Ball'. This Victorian engraving may have a distasteful title by our standards and we may doubt the motives for publication, but it provides a valuable social document. It stresses that the regime here was always benign in contrast to the workhouse.

50. Two of the hospital nurses, December 1918. This portrait was by Phillips' main rivals, Dawkes and Partridge. They were two Vicars Choral who began their business in Tucker Street, moved to High Street (where this picture was taken) and subsequently to Market Place. When cameras were rare and elaborate, portraits helped to support several photographers in Wells.

51. Brown's Gate from Cathedral Green in 1839. This was another of the three gates linking town and precinct commissioned by Bekynton, and it cost 200 marks. The property to the left (now nos. 20 and 22 Sadler Street) was part of the same project as the New Works. Before the precinct was walled the western steps were located here.

52.   No. 10 Broad Street, *c.*1900. Despite the grand name the shop is in fact a grocer's with some ironmongery and other items. Note the substantial staff then necessary for a relatively small shop. This property and its neighbours date from the 1830s, after the turnpike company had widened Wet Lane. The developer was William Charles.

COMPANY.
ORTERS.
MILD CURED BACON
JAMES NE
LIM
FOR
QUALITY
CHEAPNESS
WE
SURPASS
ALL

53. The crenellated gatehouse of the Old Deanery, the second grandest ecclesiastic's residence in Wells. Today it is a mixture of medieval and 18th-century elements. The only major change since this picture was taken some 90 years ago is that the ivy has been cleared from the walls.

54. No. 9 Cathedral Green, usually called the music school. This was another canonical house but was lost early when the Archdeacon of Wells, Polydore Vergil, fell foul of Henry VIII. It was forfeited and passed through many hands. By 1800 the building was an assembly room and brewery, but was acquired for the theological college in 1888. This shows the conversion in progress.

55. Herbert E. Balch, the founder of the museum and its honorary curator for 60 years. Balch began his working life as a postboy and ended as postmaster. His collection of fossils, minerals and archaeological remains formed the basis of the collection, which was housed in rooms over the west cloister before 1933.

56. No. 8 Cathedral Green, the modern museum. This was one of the houses granted to the canons. Half were held by the bishop and half by the Dean and Chapter, and this was one of the bishop's. It was finally sold for £396 6s. in 1828. The museum moved here in 1933.

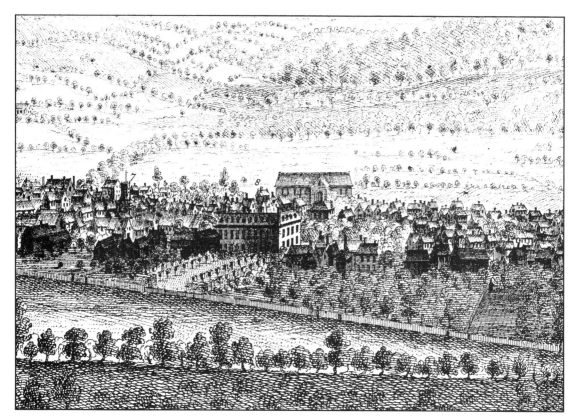

57. Chamberlain Street, from the Buck brothers' panorama of 1736. This extract shows the Coward family mansion (later the Catholic convent). Leading citizens had occupied this site since the 14th century, and in 1736 it had recently been extended westwards to incorporate three properties of the Vicars Choral. Three cottages opposite were demolished in 1720 to create a rural vista.

58. Chamberlain Street from the east. The two properties on the right are 18th-century replacements for two inns. The nearer was first the *Antelope* and, after the Restoration, the *King's Arms*. The further was the *Bear* and later the *Angel*. The block opposite dates from the 1840s. Beyond are the convent and church.

59. Chamberlain Street looking west to its junction with New Street and Sadler Street. In the Middle Ages St Helen's Cross occupied the junction. Note that the precinct wall lacked battlements before it was set back. Left-hand houses look similar but were built over a period of 50 years. A medieval hall is incorporated in no. 8, second from the camera.

60. Chamberlain Street, central section. Nos. 25-31 (odd) were known as the Limes, and this view of 1859 shows the reason. It is the last of a row of magnificent trees that stood within the bounds of the road until felled that year. The nearest house on the left was demolished when nos. 25-31 were built. The other properties survive little altered.

61. Cedar Stables, College Road, with the Tudway family wagonette, c.1897. When Charles Tudway was having The Cedars built (see pictures 73 and 74 below) he had the associated stables built across the road. The site had been a 'tenement or little house' of the vicars which was exchanged for land at Easton. The premises are now part of the Cathedral School.

62. Stoberry House was approached from the head of College Road or Bristol Hill. It was built for Peter Davis, one of the resident gentry, c.1745, the house and park occupying the site of a former medieval open field. The Sherston family acquired the estate in 1778, and they sold it to J. P. Tudway in 1854. Stoberry House was demolished just after World War Two.

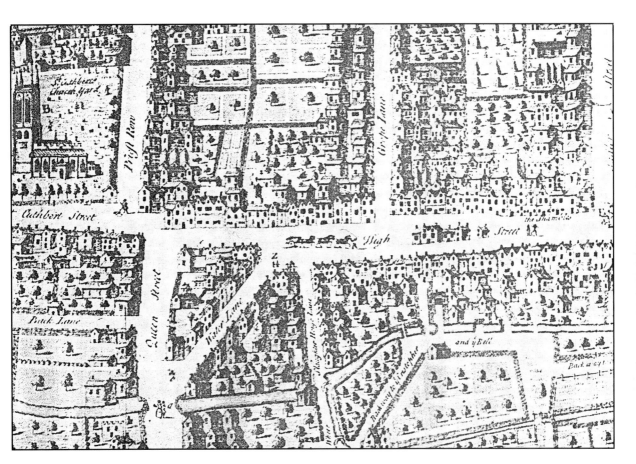

63. High Street, according to Simes. Note Middle Row, which the Corporation removed in 1768. On market days the street was further filled with stalls which even crowded the passage south of Middle Row. Also note Jacob's Well (marked Z), which survived until the mid-19th century. Before the Reformation Banner Cross adjoined it and King's Cross stood to the west of Middle Row.

64. The *Red Lion*, which has an address in High Street despite facing Market Place. This shows it while it was a temperance hotel, with a bar-like coffee room on the ground floor which was typical of the tactics employed by the local temperance movement.

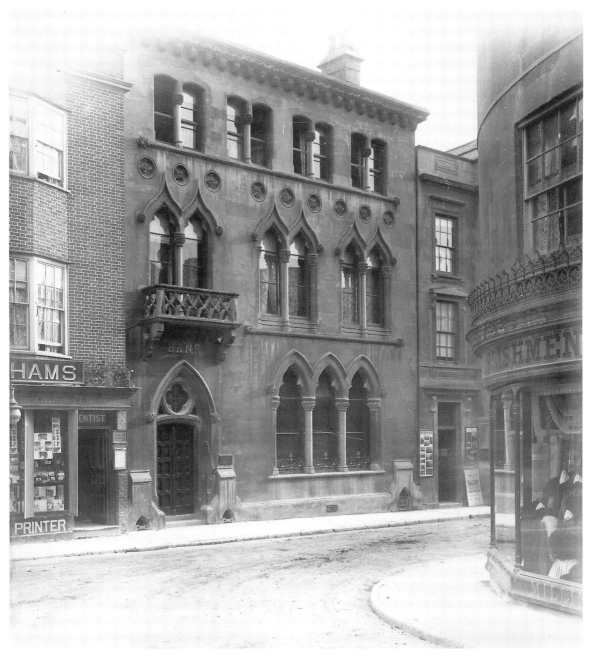

65. Stuckey's Bank, no. 7 High Street (now the National Westminster). Stuckey's was a Somerset bank that opened in Wells in 1825 at no. 9 High Street. These larger premises in gothic revival style date from 1855 and replaced the *George*. This was the best inn of early modern Wells and it can be traced back to 1388.

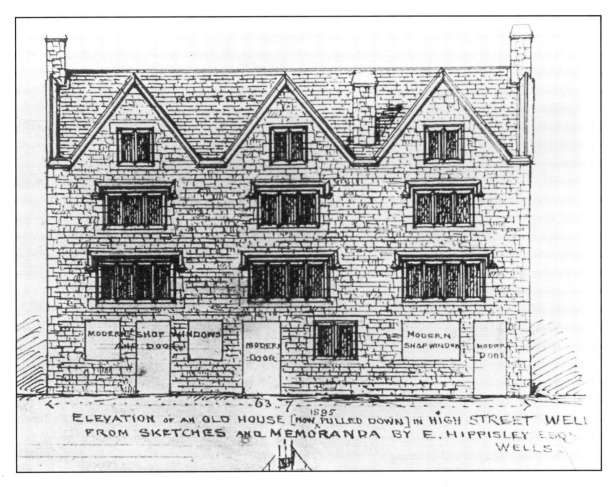

ELEVATION OF AN OLD HOUSE [NOW PULLED DOWN] IN HIGH STREET WELLS FROM SKETCHES AND MEMORANDA BY E. HIPPISLEY ESQ WELLS

66. Nos. 6 and 8 High Street were refronted in 1895, and thus have a plain brick façade, although they contain older elements, notably a fine 17th-century stair. This drawing records its previous appearance.

67. Another feature of the property was felt worthy of a postcard c.1930. By 1426 the premises were owned by the Corporation and from 1642 until c.1830 were leased by the Pearce family of bakers. The first was James, followed by five called Elias, the first of whom must have been the E on the inscribed triangular plates.

68. The central portion of High Street. The canopy on the right identifies the *Somerset Hotel*, which was an inn by 1404 and before 1862 had been named the *Christopher*. Opposite are the *King's Head* and *Star* which still survive. The temperance movement competed with the *King's Head* by opening a 'coffee tavern' next door.

69. Tyte's grocers, no. 53 High Street. Samuel Tyte first leased the premises in 1871 at £42 p.a. For over 200 years, until the 1850s, the site had been an alehouse. It was the *Cock* until 1793 and then the *King's Arms*. Before 1712 it was a butcher's shop. The Georgian façade was built during its time as the *King's Arms*.

70. Taylor's butcher's, no. 51 High Street. It has characteristic removable windows or shutters, and a display which encroached on to the space above the footway. Such displays increased at weekends and would be prodigious before Christmas. Such practices were banished only by post-Second World War health regulations.

71. The same premises a decade earlier with a full Christmas display. The encroachment on the pavement is even more blatant. A table has been placed on it to display ribs of beef which look very fat for modern tastes. Of course displaced pedestrians would have been in less danger from the traffic then.

72. Madame Rea's, no. 55 High Street, photographed *c*.1920. The premises are still a ladies-wear shop today. Until the mid-19th century Jacob's Well was in front of this property.

73. The Cedars, no. 15, The Liberty, viewed from the garden, c.1895. It was built by Thomas Paty for Charles Tudway in 1758 after the latter had inherited an Antiguan sugar plantation purchased by his great-uncle. It replaced the College of Montroy. The conservatory on the right is part of the 1866 extensions and replaced a canonical house shown in picture 40.

74. Charles Tudway (1713-70) from his portrait by Gainsborough. He inherited the plantation at Parham Hill, Antigua, in 1749. Besides building The Cedars he developed his family's political influence, being elected mayor three times and acting as one of Wells' two M.P.s in 1754.

75. Clement Tudway (1734-1815) from his portrait by Gainsborough, *c.*1764. Clement was Charles' eldest son and heir, and M.P. from 1760 to 1815. With his brothers he made the Tudway influence in Wells absolute for over 50 years. His nephew, John Paine Tudway, succeeded him and was M.P. for Wells from 1815 to 1830.

76. The Tudways left The Cedars for Milton Lodge (see picture 97) in 1909. During World War One The Cedars was used as a military hospital, and afterwards it was occupied by the theological college. This was succeeded by the Cathedral School, which bought the house in 1967. This front view was taken whilst it was in use as a hospital. Note the railings, which were removed in World War Two.

77. The drawing room of The Cedars, c.1900, with the parlour beyond. These were the dining rooms of the cathedral school from 1926 to 1985, when a new dining hall was opened behind the house. Now they are used for the reception of visitors, and administration.

78. A view of the drawing room photographed whilst The Cedars was a military hospital. The family portrait is a reminder of past glories.

79. A party of patients about to leave for Castle Cary. The happy faces and still bandaged arm indicate that this was an excursion rather than the first stage of a return to the front.

80. No. 19 The Liberty. The present house was built for the physician Claver Morris between 1699 and 1702. It cost him £807 14s. 6¾d. and was probably the first house with sash windows in Wells. Claver Morris held the site on a series of 40-year leases from the Dean and Chapter, and his daughter's descendants, the Burlands, continued to lease it until 1839.

81. Claver Morris from his memorial in the cloisters. His *Journal* survives to illustrate the life of Wells until 1726. He was a fiery little man frequently involved in disputes which often involved property. He quarrelled with Bishop Kidder over his sly wooing of Kidder's daughter and with his successor, Bishop Hooper, over a claimed right of way through Vicars' Close.

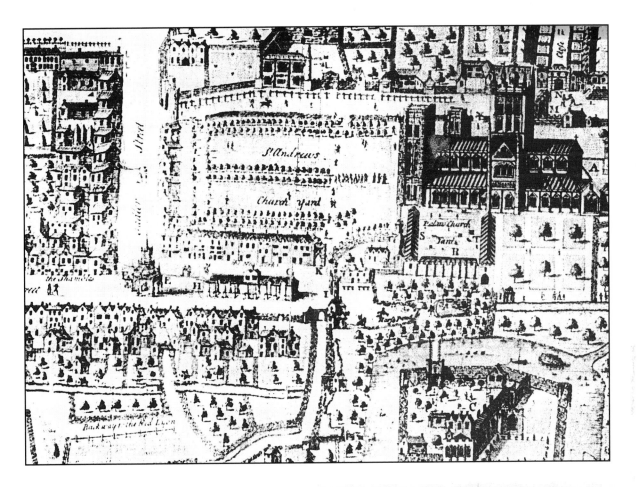

St Andrews

Church yard

82. Market Place, pictured by Simes. This shows a number of features lost soon after. They are the medieval High Cross, the Guildhall, crenellations on the New Works (which were probably original as William Worcester mentioned them *c*.1470), and the canonical house (removed in 1779). This house's garden gave the Market Place its modern L-shape.

83. The High Cross, removed 1779. This dated from the very end of the Middle Ages, being a gift from Richard Woolman (Dean 1529-37). It succeeded an earlier cross, as the shops on the site of modern no. 1 Market Place were identified as being opposite the High Cross from 1414.

84.   Market Place, *c*.1790, showing Bekynton's conduit. On the left there is a pair of houses on the Sadler Street corner. They were built *c*.1745 in a rather old-fashioned style. The further building on the south side was demolished in 1839 as it protruded in front of the Town Hall.

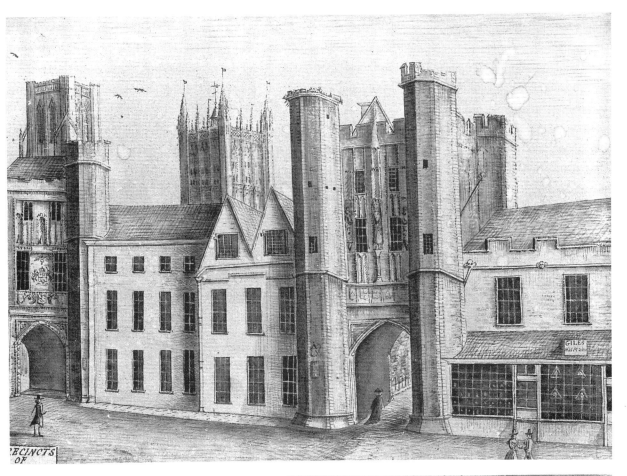

85. The eastern side of Market Place, *c.*1800. The front southern turret of the Bishop's Eye gatehouse has lost most of its battlements in the decade since the last view. Contrast the three houses (from right to left nos. 12, 14 and 16) with pictures 89 and 93 below, and with their modern form.

86. A detail from the rear of Penniless Porch. It is Bekynton's *rebus* (or badge), and shows a beacon and a barrel or tun (so Beacon-tun). This device or his more formal coat-of-arms mark his many building works. The rooms over Penniless Porch were let together with the easternmost of the New Works.

87. The town hall in its Victorian form. The ground level arches were originally open, and the cheese market was held on the ground floor while the council met above. Cheese sales moved out when the Market Hall was brought into use in 1836. The central balcony was not added until the 1920s.

88. The Market Hall (now converted to the post office) in its original open form. It was built in 1835-6 as the last town improvement by the old, unreformed council. It cost £3,269. The post office brake, which collected mailbags from the stations and undertook local transfers, is in front.

89.   Market Place in 1906, showing the 1799 replacement for Bekynton's conduit and the Russian cannon that adjoined it for nearly a century. It was one of the many Crimean War souvenirs that ornamented British towns until they were sacrificed to World War munition campaigns. On the right is the top of the sign for the *Royal Oak*, a beerhouse that shut shortly after this photograph was taken.

90.   The *Crown Inn*, c.1925. This and its eastern neighbours were a lucrative development by one of the canons who held the house which was replaced by the Town Hall. The *Crown* and neighbours replaced his side garden. The basic structure of the inn is medieval and it has certainly carried the sign of the *Crown* since the late 16th century.

MAY MARKET
WELLS
may 1st 1897

91. May Market, 1897. The animation contrasts with the empty streets that Phillips preferred for his studies. The two houses on the Sadler Street corner were replaced subsequently by the Midland Bank. Their fronts had been modernised to plain Georgian after 1790 (compare with picture 84).

92.   The *Royal Oak*. The *Crown's* neighbour and part of the same development, this was a beerhouse from 1830 to 1906. Earlier occupiers were described variously as hairdresser, barber or peruk-maker. It is now an annexe of the *Crown* known as *Penn's Bar*. This name records an occasion in 1694 when the Quaker William Penn preached from an upper window.

93.   The eastern side of Market Place, *c*.1918. Contrast with picture 85. No. 14 Market Place has lost its prominent gables but gained a front door: it was formerly entered via the Bishop's Eye; no. 12 has lost its shop-front; while neither has a crenellated parapet at this stage. The iron railings were to fall victim to wartime munition drives.

94. Phillips' photographic shop decorated for Edward VII's coronation, with Thomas Phillips on the left. The business was started in 1855 by John Budge, a cabinet-maker, whose apprentice had been Thomas Phillips. In turn Phillips was succeeded by his son Bert and the last proprietor was Bert's former assistant, Mrs. Southwood. This book would have been impossible without their work.

95. Phillips' shop had a major renovation in the 1930s. This shows work in progress, revealing the timber frame and the laths which supported the internal plaster. Note that the business has expanded since the last picture and taken over the former *Royal Oak*. That was done in 1907. Bert Phillips added no. 4 Market Place (part of the *Crown* frontage) *c*.1920.

96. New Street from Sadler Street, looking north across the site of St Helen's Cross, before the setting-back of the precinct wall. Nos. 1 and 3 (in front) replaced a row of small cottages as this area became fashionable. No. 5 New Street was an inn from the 17th to mid-18th century.

97. Charles Clement Tudway and his family moved to Milton Lodge, Old Bristol Road, in 1909. He was deeply interested in gardening, especially flowering shrubs, and he and his successors have made the gardens into a major attraction. The site is helped by a magnificent view over Wells. This photograph taken in 1970 shows the outlook from the terrace.

98. David Tudway Quilter, the present owner of Milton Lodge and grandson of C. C. Tudway, firing one of the cannons on the terrace after being made Mayor of Wells in 1974. Family involvement with the town was then into its third century. The cannons were formerly at The Cedars, and were fired at midnight when C. C. Tudway was twenty-one.

99.   Portway before World War One. Wells kept to its medieval limits until the latter part of Victoria's reign. During the early years of the new century these substantial semi-detached houses were built. Note the panes of the main windows with their gothic touches.

100.   No. 18 Priory Road decorated for Edward VII's coronation. At that time it was the home of J. Tait who is shown in the middle of the policemen in picture 148. Priory Road was laid out in 1830 but its frontage was built up very slowly. This property was constructed in 1886.

101.   Priest Row also decorated for Edward VII's coronation in 1902. This, and picture 38, give tantalising glimpses of the west side properties since demolished. The taller building was successively Wells Theatre, a non-conformist chapel and St Cuthbert's room, when it was used for events connected with the parish church.

102.   The *Swan*, Sadler Street, here decorated for Victoria's Jubilee. This is the most venerable of the surviving inns, first mentioned in 1422. Its appearance reflects a rebuilding of 1768-9. Note the double archway to the yard which has since been altered to take motor vehicles. Just glimpsed beyond is the *Swan Vaults*, an independently run beerhouse despite the name.

103.   The *Mitre*, nos. 15 and 17 Sadler Street, which had previously been at no. 13, then 20 and 22 before settling here. At this stage public house functions were sited south of the yard at no. 15 and the hotel at no. 17. The latter had previously been the *Flower de Luce* inn from 1605-*c*.1760. The *Mitre* coach is shown here approaching its destination, *c*.1890.

104.   The *White Hart*, Sadler Street. This has been an inn since 1497, and was originally the *Hart's Head*. The *White Hart* sign was transferred from Market Place *c.*1700. This photograph shows an excursion about to set out, while behind the group may be seen the original plain Georgian façade and also its southern neighbour, a beerhouse called the *Nag's Head*.

105. The *White Hart* transformed, *c*.1908. The *Nag's Head* has been demolished. Most of its site has formed a yard but the *White Hart* has been extended southwards. It has gained half-timbering and two gables. Note the street beyond: the precinct wall beyond Brown's Gate has been set back since this photograph was taken, to widen the road and create a pavement.

106. Nos. 23 and 25 Sadler Street from Brown's Gate, *c*.1930. Eating and drinking places have always crowded along the western boundary of the Liberty of St Andrew. From 1500 to 1800 there were inns and taverns. More recently cafés and restaurants have appeared. Planning controls on listed buildings and conservation areas have since reduced the exuberance of advertising.

107. The flank of no. 16 Sadler Street. The roof shows how this property and its neighbours were built in two parts straddling the precinct wall. This was reflected in ownership: the front was leased from the bishop and the rear from the Dean and Chapter. Furthermore, the former leased for three named lives but the latter for 40-year periods.

108. No. 3 St Andrew Street, known as the Rib or the Bishop's Rib. The latter name reflects its status as one of the bishop's canonical houses. It clearly shows its origins as a medieval hall house. From 1862 it was occupied by the principal of the theological college. When that was transferred to Salisbury it passed to the Cathedral School.

109. St Cuthbert Street, *c*.1775. This street had been an area where rich merchants lived in the late 13th and early 14th centuries. Then it declined steadily and here looked decidedly rustic with thatch and unmade road. Soon after, a revival began. The cottages on the Portway corner were redeveloped by 1797. Note the mature trees in the churchyard which were lost to Victorian improvement.

110. The west end of St Thomas Street with St Andrew Street and the cathedral beyond from a water-colour of 1839. It shows the *Fountain Inn*, no. 1, St Thomas Street. That inn had moved to its present site from the corner of St Andrew Street and The Liberty in 1810. The only major changes in 150 years have concerned the buildings beyond Tor Street.

111. A view from marginally further up St Thomas Street, *c*.1900. This is a characteristic study by Dawkes and Partridge who favoured romantic scenes. Exteriors were often misty or, as here, taken at dusk. Interiors have shafts of sunlight. Perhaps they had to differentiate themselves from the Phillips' manner. This was entitled 'Nocturne'.

112. The *Lamb* and (on the left) the *Somerset Inn*, St Thomas Street. The latter had the longer history having been the *East Wells Inn* until 1822 and then the *Exmouth*. It adopted its final name in 1887 following the closure of the *Somerset Hotel* in High Street. All the properties shown now have front boundary walls and, space allowing, gardens.

113. Eastern Wells from the cathedral tower, *c.*1895. The Liberty is on the left lined by canonical houses. On the right St Andrew and St Thomas Streets lead up to St Thomas' church. Points to note include Stoberry Park in the left background and the inn signs of the *Fountain*, *Goat*, *Lamb*, and *Coach and Horses*.

114. The ford in Silver Street, *c*.1830. This road only had frontage development from *c*.1800. Previously it provided a rear access to Southover and South Street properties and the way to the bishop's barn. The stream was part of an elaborate system of waterways shown in the next illustration, acting as an overflow from the millstreams.

115. The water-courses in 1735. St Andrew's Stream or the millstream flows along the southern boundaries of High Street properties to drive the two wheels of the In-mill at Mill Street. Surplus water could be diverted south to meet a second stream from Palace Mill and they filled a second horsepool which gave South Street its old name of Lawpool Lane.

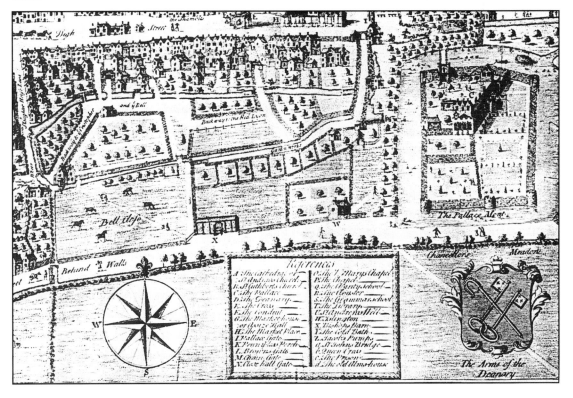

116. Southover showing nos. 2-36 (even), in the mid-1950s. This was the appearance of working-class Wells. The further properties were removed to make a council development, Beckett Place. The nearer houses survived but have been reorientated to open on to the Place. Their former front doors are blocked.

117. Foster's Court, Southover. This is a survival of the lower priced working-class houses which were strung along alleys running back into the long plots of Southover and St Thomas Street. It looks pleasant now but originally these courts had minimal sanitation and faced the blank rear wall of their neighbour. Most were cleared by the council after the Second World War.

118. The Methodist church, Southover. The first non-conformist chapel in Wells was established on this site in 1738 but it was Presbyterian. It was being used by the Methodists by 1817, and the chapel was enlarged by them. They enlarged it in 1838 and 1865. The interior was redecorated in the 1950s and this picture records the reopening. Mrs. Southwood (of Phillips') is fifth from the left.

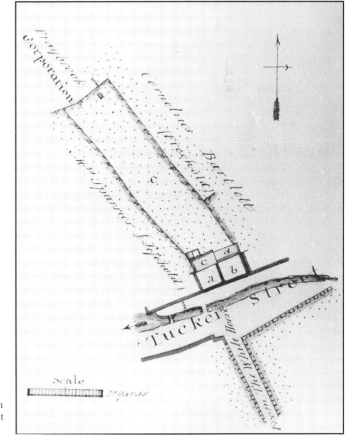

119. Tucker Street in 1821, showing the last unculverted portion of the Ludbourne. This stream rose in the Combe, one branch running down New Street and another along College Road and The Liberty. The combined waters flowed along Chamberlain Street and on to Tucker Street. The plan is from a Corporation survey and shows properties lost to the railway.

120. Stage coach in Market Place, *c.*1800. This must have been a London to Exeter mail coach which called daily (1 p.m. eastbound and 2 p.m. westbound). Local coaches to Bath, Taunton and Exeter departed from the *Swan* with an additional service to Bath from the *Christopher*. Carriers' wagons were based at the *Star*, *White Hart* and *Mitre*. The architectural detail shown here is unreliable.

121. 'The triumph of the 19th century': Sadler Street decorated for the arrival of the railway in 1859. This and picture 60 are the oldest surviving photographs of Wells that have been traced. Despite the horse making a symbolic exit left, horses were to remain the predominant form of local transport for a further half-century.

122.   The *Swan* coach, *c.*1890. As the railway stations were peripheral the major inns (the *Swan*, the *Star* and the *Mitre*) had coaches to ferry passengers to and from the trains. On the strength of this link the *Star* was entered as the *Star and Railway Hotel* in the 1859 Directory.

123. Those nearer to the stations also tried to capitalise. This is no. 33 Southover. It had been a beerhouse since 1839 but was now named the *Railway Tavern* although it was 300 yards from the stations. Similarly the present *Sherston Hotel* which adjoined them became the *Railway Hotel*. The tavern's earlier name – the *Travellers Rest* – is still displayed over one door.

124. The *Railway Tavern* closed in the 1960s but its interior was renovated some 10 years before. This shows the regulars celebrating the completion of the works. Third from the right is Harry Paul, proprietor of W. & H. Paul and much in demand as a sign-writer. The various World War Two campaign signs were his creations (see pictures 151-3).

125.   The S. & D.J.R. station viewed from the level crossing with that company's signal box on the left. This picture was taken after the closure which occurred in 1951 before the Beeching axe. When operational a canopy extended over both platform and train with a wall beyond so that the whole rather resembled an engine shed.

126.   A view from the signal box showing the S. & D.J.R. goods yard. This was spacious with a shed and crane. It continued to be used in connection with Tucker Street after the closure of the Glastonbury line. The G.W.R. line runs in from the left. They paid the S. & D.J.R. £400 p.a. for the right to use nine chains (594 ft.) of track.

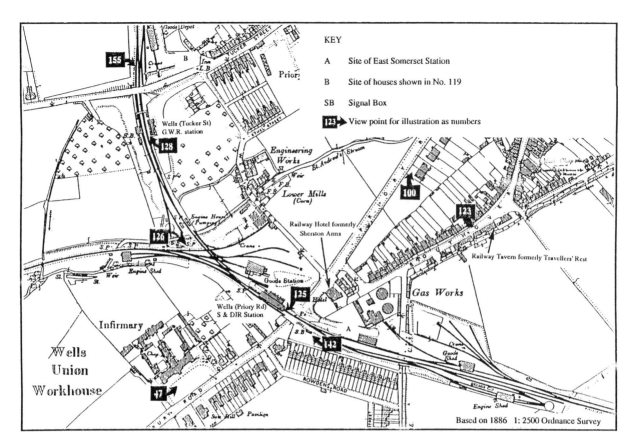

KEY

A   Site of East Somerset Station

B   Site of houses shown in No. 119

SB   Signal Box

123➤   View point for illustration as numbers

Based on 1886 1: 2500 Ordnance Survey

127. An extract from the first detailed Ordnance Survey map of 1886 showing the various railway layouts and related developments. The *Railway Hotel*, as mentioned, was no new development. It originally faced Southover and was rearranged after 1830 to front Priory Road. Previously the hotel had been the *Black Bull*, *White Horse*, and *Sherston Arms*.

128. Tucker Street station. The G.W.R. station was a grander affair than its rival with two platforms and a linking pedestrian bridge. This photograph was taken during World War Two and records a scheme whereby local families entertained Australian servicemen, two of whom are about to leave.

129. R. C. Cock, a local builder, in his trap in Market Place, *c*.1910.

130. A coach outside the town hall, *c*.1900. Coaches were used on formal occasions by judges, mayors, sheriffs and lords lieutenant and they persisted well into the age of motor vehicles to give reminders of past styles. The uniforms of the coachman and attendants also make statements about civic pride and prestige. (For the sheriff's coach see picture 147.)

131. This was probably the first car based in Wells as it occasioned a Phillips' postcard, which dates from *c*.1905. The pressure of traffic was obviously slight as it could be parked across New Street for the study. The street is little changed except for parking controls.

132. An early motorised excursion about to leave Market Place before World War One. Those involved would probably have called this splendid vehicle a charabanc.

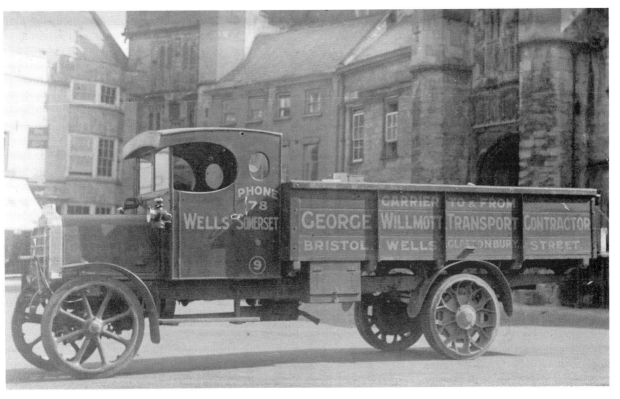

133. The first Wells-owned lorry parked in an otherwise empty Market Place. The telephone was also very new. Note the two digit telephone number.

134. An early motor-cycle combination, again probably just before World War One.

135. Buses and the local crews in Market Place, 1921. Note the hierarchical arrangement. The inspector is seated centrally and is identified by both cap and the officer-style braid on his sleeves. The drivers are on either side and behind him. The younger conductors form the edges of the group. The two on the bench are perched at its ends.

136. The Cottage Hospital ambulance and nurses, *c*.1918. The Cottage Hospital was located at the eastern end of St Thomas Street. It only had two small wards – one for men and the other for women, so its own ambulance seems something of a luxury. However, the nurses probably came from the Cedars Military Hospital judging from their red crosses.

137. A car rally in Market Place, *c*.1928. The two nearer vehicles are Morris Oxfords.

138. Wells City Garage, no. 29 Broad Street in the early 1920s with an array of vehicles and appropriately dressed drivers. A photograph was still a major event – note the children watching from the first floor of no. 27 (to the left).

139.   Harry Paul's first car, late 1920s, and photographed outside W. & H. Paul's premises at no. 2, St Cuthbert Street, immediately to the west of the churchyard.

140.   Tradesmen's delivery vehicles were usually muscle-powered until after 1945. These two dairy tricycles caught the trade at a time of major change. Ruff was still operating in the old way, the milk being in churns from which it was ladled into customers' jugs or bottles, while Searle had switched to bottled milk.

141.   Royal limousine 1944. Queen Mary is being driven into the palace grounds at the start of a Royal visit. School children line the way but wartime austerity has left them without flags to wave.

142.   The latter days of the railway at Wells. An ex-G.W.R. pannier tank on the turntable with the G.W.R signal box behind. This box was built to control the Priory Road crossing. Parts of the crossing gate, the closed S.& D.J.R. station and the S.& D.J.R. signal box can be glimpsed beyond. This photograph was taken in May 1959.

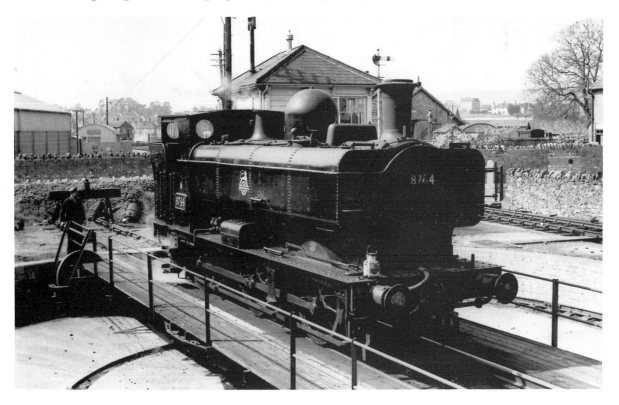

143. Empire Day 1905. It is often said that ceremonial events helped hold the medieval town together, and the Wells records reveal the survival of guild entertainments and May Day shows into the early 17th century. However, this and following pictures illustrate a rich tradition of civic ceremony which only declined after the middle of this century. This is a typical scene.

144. A view looking the other way to the last. Empire Day was regularly celebrated as a major occasion until World War Two. Its ingredients were bands, parades and speeches. Note the platform erected outside the Town Hall for the speakers and other dignitaries.

145.   A mayoral procession, probably 1903. They are leaving Market Place and the most likely destination is St Cuthbert's church. The mayor is accompanied by the town clerk and preceded by the City maces. The councillors follow in top hats. All appear vastly overdressed to us as it is obviously a sunny summer day.

146. A church parade, again in 1905. Note the troops' wide-brimmed hats, appropriate dress for those whose recent active duty had been in South Africa and the north-west frontier of India. In the background is an excellent view of the house which was to become the museum.

147. Wells was an assize town until 1970, which added further ceremonies, such as special services at the cathedral. It also drew county dignitaries to Wells and explains the presence of the Sheriff's coach outside the Town Hall *c.*1900. It is similar to the coach in picture 130 but details differ; for example, the position of the lamps.

148.   The assize filled the town. Amongst those drawn to it were policemen. As a result Phillips was able to record the constabulary of the entire Glastonbury division in 1896. It was probably a good day for poachers and other petty offenders in the rest of the area!

149. After the delirious joy of Armistice Day there was a more organised and sober celebration of peace the following year. This is certainly the largest crowd recorded by either Phillips and it seems remarkably still.

150. Between the wars Prebendary E. B. Cook revived May Day ceremonies for the local school children, which included Maypole dancing and the election of a May queen. This photograph shows children in costume. George Paul, mounted on the pony, is May prince.

151.   Both World Wars were characterised by a succession of drives, appeals and campaigns. War Weapons Week was a typical example from World War Two. Parades and speeches were vital ingredients.

152.   Wings for Victory Week with Harry Paul posed in front of an example of his sign-writing. After the War he was able to turn his talents to restoration, working first on the Jacobean Royal Arms from St Cuthbert's. Then in 1959, assisted by his son George, he restored the quarter-jacks from the cathedral.

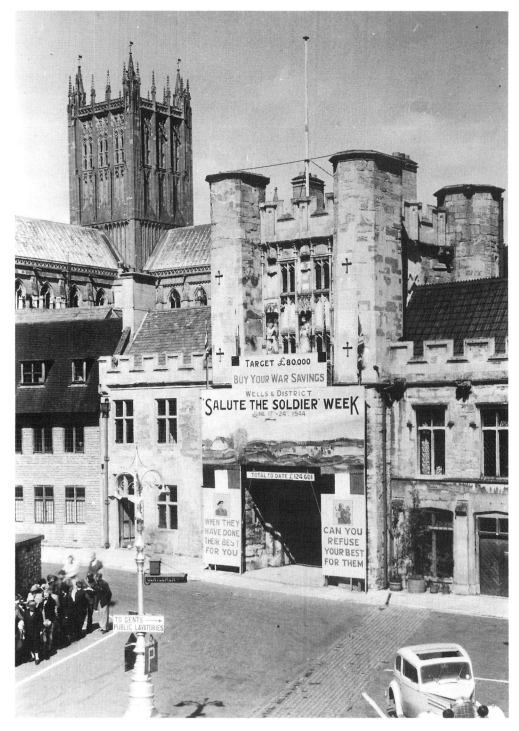

TARGET £80.000
BUY YOUR WAR SAVINGS
WELLS & DISTRICT
'SALUTE THE SOLDIER' WEEK
JUNE 17 - 24th 1944

TOTAL TO DATE £ 124.601

WHEN THEY
HAVE DONE
THEIR BEST
FOR YOU

CAN YOU
REFUSE
YOUR BEST
FOR THEM

TO GENTS
PUBLIC LAVATORIES

153. Support the Soldier Week is a further example. This view also records the brief existence of a brick-built air raid shelter in Market Place. The queue of people beside it is not anticipating an emergency. This was the picking-up point for buses in the war years.

154.   A salvage drive was another typical World War event. Here the greatest success seems to have been in collecting the local lads. Note that no. 16, Market Place (behind) has finally assumed its modern form, in contrast to pictures 85 and 93.

155. Even the collected scrap metal needed a formal send off from a party which included the mayor and senior railwaymen, with the proceedings recorded by Bert Phillips. The train is in the Tucker Street goods yard with Burcott Road bridge beyond. The banners state 'clear out scrap – it all helps win the war'.

156. Admiral Somerville commanded the force which pursued and sank the German battleship *Bismarck*. In 1944 he was granted the Freedom of the City of Wells. Here he is shown flanked by civic dignitaries. There was the inevitable accompaniment of military parades and speeches.

157. The end of World War Two provided a final opportunity for military parades. Here the A.T.S. wait to play their part.

158. The audience for the 1945 celebrations, women and children predominating in the crowd.

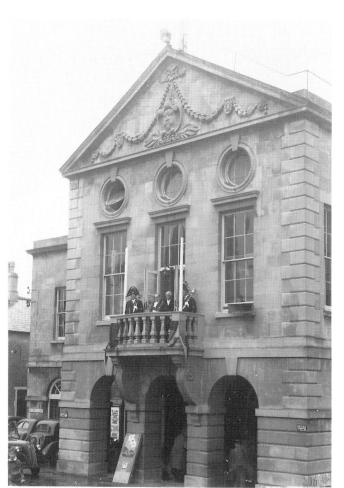

159. Postwar austerity kept campaign weeks alive for some years. This is Savings Week, October 1949. Note how the addition of a balcony to the Town Hall transformed civic ceremony by both elevating and limiting the number of dignitaries. Contrast with picture 88 for other architectural changes.

160. A more relaxed approach to events in the 1970s. Mayor David Tudway Quilter leads a sponsored walk in the palace grounds. Bishop 'Jock' Henderson is amongst those following. By this time Mendip District Council had been created and Wells had lost the self-government which had been built up between 1166 to 1589. Nevertheless, the atmosphere contrasts sharply with the scenes above.

161. The carnival has been a great and enduring ceremony in Wells throughout the century. Here a gang of men is collecting wood for the 1905 bonfire.

162. One of the floats for the 1905 procession. Recording peoples' carnival costumes provided an important part of Phillips' livelihood. The studio stayed open to midnight on carnival night.

163.   The completed bonfire in the recreation ground, 1902. The construction of this towering structure with strategically placed tar barrels required expert supervision. Note how everybody has dressed formally for this official record, in contrast to the shirt sleeves of picture 161.

164. A prize-winning float, *c.*1910. This was the best decorated two-wheeled vehicle of the year. It is photographed in the *Mitre* yard which was a base for local carriers; hence the parcel room.

165. An early Phillips picture of a carnival costume – Harry Paul in 1902. This was sent in the post and the message records that his car (i.e. float), 'The Knighting of Drake', received second prize while he obtained third prize for his ball costume.

166. After 1920 cars became a regular feature of the carnival. Here one is almost totally disguised. While the earlier pictures were taken by daylight, this and subsequent photographs were generally taken by flash during the procession. Bert Phillips and Mrs. Southwood now had early (unreliable) equipment, which involved magnesium powder on a tray which was fired at, or above, head level.

WELLS FIRE BRIGADE

167.   The local fire brigade was an essential part of the carnival and other processions. Here the brigade is shown about to join the 1928 carnival with helmets and fire-engine gleaming. Their predecessors had participated with horse-drawn vehicles.

168. Floats were always accompanied by costumed walkers, who were better placed to collect money. These matching inter-war costumes were recorded in a studio portrait by Dawkes and Partridge.

169. Mechanical haulage resulted in a steady increase in the size of the floats; this was big for 1932. At that time the procession not only toured the historic nucleus but visited the Cottage Hospital via The Liberty, North Road and St Thomas Street. This barely turned the North Road corner just as modern leviathans have trouble with the corner of High Street and Sadler Street.

170. Women's rights are not an entirely new issue. Membership of the bowls club was obviously a topical matter in 1937. This seems strange today in a town which had supported a women's football team in the 1920s.

171. Modern carnival. Floats have been transformed by the successive impact of the internal combustion engine, taped music and the combination of generator and electric light bulbs. Most floats now come from organisations or specialist clubs. Members work for months and large sums are spent on materials. The results are seen for only a few days on the Somerset carnival circuit.

172. In contrast the individual costumed walkers are far closer to early carnivals. Although the costumes vary from year to year, depending on what is topical, the enjoyment of the spectators is constant.

173. Wells has always supported a wide range of sports teams. Some have been orthodox like bowls, cricket and football while others have represented local specialities. This is the local football team at the end of the 1893-4 season when they had won the Challenge Cup.

174. Quoits is more of a local interest but it was very popular in the years around 1900. This is shown by the number of pictures surviving and the existence of more than one club. This is the St Thomas Quoits Club of 1908. Note that the actual quoits were massive.